*mah*cic

selected **poems**

tomás**riley**

calaca press
national city, califas
2005

Several poems presented previously appeared in: *Bum Rush The Page: A Def Poetry Jam* (Three Rivers), *Chorizo Tonguefire: The Taco Shop Poets Anthology* (Chorizo Tonguefire), *Pacific Review* (San Diego State U Press), *Tea Party Magazine* (Oakland), two chapbooks by the author *My Peoples Are You With Me?* and *Message From the New Forreal*, and in audio form on *Chorizo Tonguefire* (Calaca), *Intersections* (Chorizo Tonguefire) and *Message From the New Forreal* (Self-Release).

 Published by Calaca Press
P.O. Box 2309, National City, Califas 91951
www.calacapress.com
calacapress@cox.net

Calaca Press is a Chicano family-owned small publishing house dedicated to publishing and producing unknown, emerging, and established progressive Chicano and Latino voices.

Design / Layout / Photos by Tomás Riley
Author cover photo by Guillermo A. Nericcio García
About the Author photo by Leticia Hernández

ISBN # 0-9717035-4-X
Library of Congress Catalog Card Number: Pending

Hecho en Aztlán
c/s

Para Mahcíc Emilio and Leticia Hernández Linares

Contents

Part 4
Mahcic

Mahcic:
A Mexipino Genealogy

mah•cic (ma-seek') [*Nahuatl*] adj. Something whole or complete.

INTRODUCTION

Being an Introduction to a Book by Tomás Riley

Guillermo "Memo" Nericcio García
y William A. Nericcio

1 The Road Less Travelled

mahcic--already, from the start, before we begin, we are faced with a choice. Robert Frost redux—the road not taken, *calles no usados*, streets, paths, odysseys—winding asphalt veins barred or barring *caminos* untraveled. "*mahcic*" takes us down two roads. One: the son; Tomás Riley's son, conceived of the poet and writer/wife Leticia even as the recombinant DNA of this book in your hands was being forged. This Mahcic is "American," born in the hallways of California Pacific Medical Center in San Francisco in 2004. The other: the book, *mahcic*, published by Calaca Press in 2005—Calaca the midwife. This other *mahcic* is "American," and Mexican, and Chicano, *y de califas*; born in the semiotic and semantic undergrowth of SoCal dude, the Southland sir, *y en Aztlán* (insert nahuatl greeting of your choice). Born at the same time: Mahcic and *mahcic*—both precious and priceless. Both filled with the blood of the [br]other. So, then, maybe, no choice. One and the same, Mahcic and *mahcic*.

2. Blind introductions

Poetry does not always grab my ears and poets almost never grab my eyes. I was born with tin-*orejas* and *ojos ciegos*—tin-ears and blind eyes plaguing this Tejano with aesthetic impediments of a sort of serious nature—after all, my day job is as a Professor of English at a California university, and if the Profs don't love poetry, if the academics ain't channeling all things literary, then Houston, we have a problem.

iii

But with Tomás Riley, my friend, my student, my advisee, my partner in crime (many hats he and I have worn and shared), the ears opened up and the eyes burned new holes through the shallow skin covering them over—something got through, he got through—and I think that those of you who carefully make your way through the delicious odyssey of these pages, you, too, will experience a new predicament as new "sounds," "visions," "scenes" and "sites" burn their way into your synapses and teach you (even as they pleasure you) a new way to be. Literature can do that to you—as surely as a lover.

3. BeforeWords
Slide past this intro already. Come back when you're finished with this book—if you are holding this in some cool indy bookstore, make the owner happy; Riley won't complain either. These words get in the way—they delay the music of a gifted muse whose ear for words and soul for lyric deserve the adoring ⟨👂⟩s of multitudes and the indulgent and attentive focus of the sentient bodies they are attached to…

4. The Life of Reilly
Riley's life of Riley—the "life of Riley" is an American colloquial phrase of Irish-American origin; it's used to refer to someone living the good life, the rich life, the life of someone born with a silver spoon in their mouth, with the tuxedoed butler bringing things, waiting on him or her hand and foot. The *life of Riley* as it unfolded for the writer Riley, Tomás or Tommy, as his friends call him, is another life. Rich, but not rich *bling bling* rich. Not poor either. Its riches derive from the semantic, musical and semiotic experimentation born from an artist who is not born and raised swimming in money. You don't have to be born poor to be a great poet, but it sure can help you some.

5. The poems
In *mahcic* we prowl the gritty streets of San Diego, the urban expanses of San Francisco—in the streets, in the barrio, with Riley we cruise rich landscapes filled with asphalt anthems, sidestreet songs and alley allusions. Riley begins his book with a prayer disguised as an epigraph, a reverie that unfolds with the cadence of the Oxford English Dictionary.

In the rich finery of standard dictionary English, Riley writes: "mah • cic (ma seek') [*Nahuatl*] adj. Something whole or complete." His epigraph prepares us for what follows in his poems—English punctuation brackets "[ ]" try to cage the *nahuatl*, but it breaks out all the same. *mahcic* breaks out, and shouts out, and we are all the richer for it. We live the life of Riley "hearing" Riley sing us his songs of Califas—collisions of image and syntax that are both poignant and delicious.

6. *Cuando ganamos*

The sad truth of it is that we don't win that often. Born, living, dying—it all comes and goes too fast. Thankfully, most of us are too dumb, dense, or stupid to know this—but poets, they know this all too well; and Riley, one of their blesséd ilk, knows this too.

With him, we watch Socrates "holding a vial / at 24th and mission," watch longer and fight, even, as we try to "find the pit of fruitless searches / for beginnings / but fruit's not gonna fall."

Hopeless, right? Not at all, for the sweet song of Riley's words act as a soul-salve, easing the pain in the limbo of our day to day now. We want to look away, you and I. We do. Because the pain of the scenes that unfold night after night in our streets etches a brooding tragedy that is tough to stomach if alluring to witness. Riley writes:

they'll take their crumpled tickets home tonight
the numbers
plucked
from memories and shame
tonight
someone behind a tv tray
within a damp apartment
will tune in to anticipate
the call of
birthdates
children's ages
days since their arrival
street addresses
fake social security numbers
saints days
bible passages
years when they were happy.

Riley writes. We listen. And what we hear and see and live (if we care to) is the tragic opera of Mexicans and other Latinos living in the enchanted spaces of a Southern California urban miasma.

Miasmas are not all bad. Strange organic beasts walk forth out of their riches to tell the tale of those who live within. And those who get out.

Riley got out. And then, magically, he went right back in. Poet, writer, educator, teacher, mentor, Riley's words and Riley's works enrich the heady spaces of the barrios he's lived in and *lived* in; they enrich the cultural cityspaces he inhabits as well.

With "mission redux" Riley's readers enter a wonderful ode to the city of San Francisco filled with evocative reveries and childhood visions. Nostalgia drenches the page with its potent, intoxicating elixirs, "ephemera that shimmers / on the glassy eyes of children / running raging / into no one's dying light."

Our Chicano troubadour does all our communities a service, authoring elegies for elided dreams; "emerging wings / already clipped" he writes, and his pen reveals the lived and living nightmare of Mexican-American and Latino US communities where more than half of the children drop or are pushed out of schools, where poverty is everyone's old friend, crack beckons, and prostitutions of all sorts hover round like helicopters with searchlights.

Our guide is a good friend. He makes us feel safe in the midst of our nightmare—that's not an easy thing to do. We walk in these pages with Tomás Riley, he playing Virgil to our Dante (though, he, the poet is more Dante than we'll ever be), *caminando*, walking streets where "cholos in waiting / mouthed the lyrics of the matrix / separating seed from need / hearts beating in the new now / time signature / a waltz of whirling leaves / across gray concrete". These words from "palmer way schoolyard hit and run," yet another poem, burning with the force of Riley's wiley heart, evoke the contours of a city scene all too familiar, but rendered new in the sly cadence of his lyric wisdom.

7. Dictionaries, Encylopedias etc.
They don't make the kind of dictionary you are going to need to read some of Riley's poems. Imagine T.S. Eliot and Billie Holiday and Jacques Derrida and Cesar Chavez and Frida Kahlo having a baby, and you begin to get a sense of the genetic density and richness of Riley's poetry.

His "rice paper wrapped recuerdos" have the power of a virus. Take, for instance, "a psalm for willie jones," which is a literary critic's wetdream. Here are some of my notes: 1."let the news come quiet as its kept"; "quiet as its kept"—Riley's first lines ape the first lines of Toni Morrison's THE BLUEST EYE; what is he trying to do? 2. "*a love supreme.*" 1964. John Coltrane. Classic jazz—how does Coltrane's epic album relate to the tragedy of Willie Jones…3. "red and black," now Riley's onto Stendahl! French literature! enough… He's deep, this Riley; he plumbs the souls of wounded city ghosts and channels their pain and vision doing what poets have always done, transforming angst and sweat and blood into beautiful art, visionary epics for new true now. Riley's epic lyrics chronicle the non-epic mundane realities of low-rent mediocrity; simultaneously he outs the heroic real-ness of the on-the-surface "nobodies" of the street and the city. Every hood has its music, every village its town crier. The backbeat of the California street finds its evocative guide in the pen of this young gifted sage. And he's got respect; in "gray grease," Riley maps the diastrophic movement, the eternal evolution of Chicana/o Arts from the movimiento to the post-movimiento; at once he tips his hat to his spiritual predecesor and, yet, also at once, gently, signals his *diferance* from his shamanic elders.

8. What He Does That Few Other Writers Do

With Riley, all is in the fusion, the coming together of languages, ideas, images and scenes that usually stay nicely segregated in books and academe. Check out these lines from "the movement: freestyles for the dying sun":

mariachi muse(sic) riffs
against the twilight of an Olmec head nod
hands fly flecha fast
to dominate the plate
rotating in the dark
obsidian outcast on the remix
overrun by selva sagrada
con su machete
en la mano mascarada

"*nosotros,*
hombres y mujeres
íntegros y libres,
estamos conscientes
de que la guerra que declaramos
es una medida última
pero justa"

Riley's lines are dense! So much to do! Aesthetes will want to focus on the controlled coming together of English and Spanish, perhaps; or, maybe, the nuanced tempo shift that occurs mid-stanzas as the poetic backbeat shifts to Spanish. Chicano studies devotees, alternatively, might want to focus on Riley's introduction of quotations from Zapatista movement declarations, signaling Riley's continued articulation of a cross-border alliance between indigenous Mexican political activist movements and Chicano lefty doings here to the north in Aztlán. Latin American studies fetishists might want to leave the aesthetes and the Chicana/o vatos to one side and focus on the Aztec iconography, the "obsidian outcasts" Riley weaves into his lyrics/lines, while American Literature Professors, eschewing all of the above, might want to grapple with their monolingual confusion confronting Riley's curious code-switching. I say, do ALL and NONE of the above. Read the poems aloud, or better yet, listen to Riley performing his monologues live AFTER reading this book, and then, let the seductive, haunting rhythms of his act redecorate the corridors of your brain. It's fun and a cheap, safe, high!

9. Riley

photo: Guillermo Nericcio García

It is 2003 and Tomás Riley is about to give a presentation to a university seminar at San Diego State University. Look at him there lurking to the left: the intensity of the gaze, the profundity of the soul—he's seen a lot in his few years on the planet and what he's seen and what he's lived have placed him in the unique position of poetic sage, with the power to move us through his manipulation and play with these little black marks on the page here in front of you. His mother a typewriter, his father an ipod; his mother wax, his father an ethernet download, between 20th and 21st century, America and Mexico, English and Spanish, Tomás Riley emerges to what should be the sustained applause of thousands of readers. The measured words, muted growls, growling musings and perfect pitches you will find in these pages have the power to leave readers on another plane, another place, and another tiempo.

Read him carefully. If you do, you won't be the same person you were when you picked up this little book, this little tasty bicultural explosive wrapped in silk, ready to blow the blindness from your eyes and kiss the small of your hearing ear.

San Diego, London y Laredo, 2005

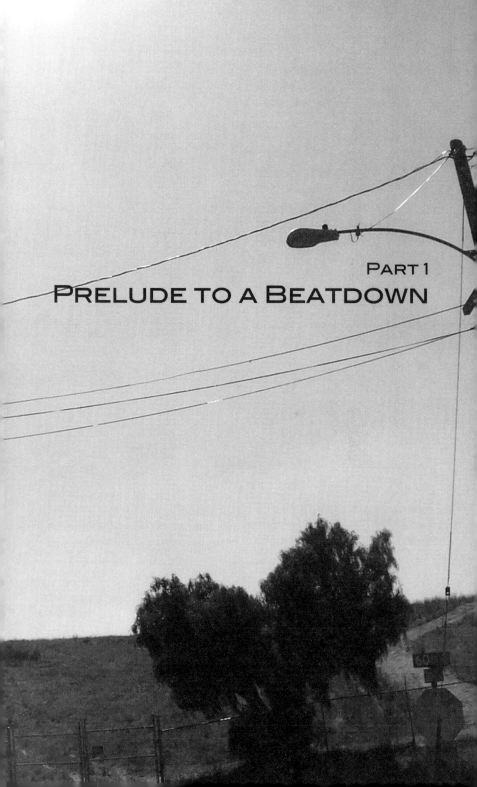

PART 1

PRELUDE TO A BEATDOWN

TWO O'CLOCK PARK JAMS:
ALL THINGS BEING SEPARATE BUT EQUAL

sometimes
when the migrant breeze
coronets
through continents
and I can see
the limp and acrid playground
emerald hills
succumb to

"foolio!
       yo, foolio!"

more bounce booming passed
the rattled chains like broken glass
now see that ass
drop
like a twenty foot bank shot.

sometimes
when i get open
and really, really hear
the infant smiles of morenitos
hanging off the fringe
on moms' daisy dukes
and the brown black
       tone dialectic
of the down beat here
and the banda over there
dangling
like the ticket
off a toe

sometimes
when i get open:

hey new jack!
hey brotha' love!
hey papi!
hey!

3

"man, i don't know you.
what you poppin
all that rah-rah for?"

and i say
nothing
i come correct
with culture
with rice paper wrapped
recuerdos
arroz con
butter beans and cornbread

and the front door
is open
soothing the hot concrete
on heated
trifling
summer afternoons
when the neighborhood kids
play freeze tag
(then grow up frozen when it's over)

sometimes
when the last of true big brothers
schools these young bucks
to my music
man, i get
wide!

sometimes
sometimes
then i can almost feel
sleep medicine
careening down the driveways
making tight
and small
the noise of children
squeezing
in

sometimes
i try to raise my fist

but get
one finger
rest it on my lips
and whisper
sssshhhhhhhh

the giant
is
sleeping

GRAY GREASE
FOR RAÚLRSALINAS

salinas slides
gray grease
against the groove
the hard
roots rock
he walks
a moment
crystal city clear
still bringing
jazz and jams again

sonrisas
tumbling
lingua franca
in a dice shoot
dipping days
salinas cool
viejito haze
'mano may raise
in riffs

he started breathing in san anto
brought it blessed in san anto
in the bop unbroken
guadalupe sunday
growing largo
salinas
dealing su descarga
and the smoke is in the air
disappearing
like a mingus moon
balloon

salinas
when they sing the sad corridos
do they also sing for you?
above the freeways passing over
and the sometimes quiet corners
we demeaned

by quarantine
the en masse
gente de masa

tired because
restlessness
is next to joblessness
and talking
the fruition of dead president cutbacks

tired because
double barrels
aim down broadway
emblematic of
i-say-so
blue clad predators

tired because
life does not
flash before the eyes
of hard rock vatos
dancing
green back mambos
celebrating every day
as día de los muertos

now die, just die
no requiems
no peace in campo santo lies
no real magic mantra may revive
conscience
not common
sense of the shaman
distant drum songs keeping time
we're running blind
holding bandanas
and bullets
and borderlines

we seek
we climb
we only find
the gristle and gray smoke sage

trencitas in the ancient way
burning down a desert stage
the migrant phrases
each by each
the whole of soul
frozen on an empty afternoon

NADA

el centro
steals color
markets voices
harvests looted rice
despite rice

bones ache
shake
raw chipotle fingers
clutching
cali-max bag purses
squatting
hard tortilla shade
on sticky black tarmacs
bright clock towers reign

> awake!
> ¡alarma!

narrow street faros
mark high noon
hissing
persecuting light and heat
diffusing yellow cab rows
and block songs
shift away
> an ocean
> the border
> and profits

bargain bin crowds
scatter flowered breezes
like bad angels
through the station
my thin joints
are worn
slanted soul
rolled over to the sun
avoiding
market street converts

outreaching
victory:

i've been blessed, ese
don't let pride be your guide

walkman jams
fade
shorty's X t-shirt message

takin' the train
takin' the train

eastbound line

through blood
            color and skin

hawking this bona fide broke doll yawning
almond shaped eyes
her attitude
the blase blah
watch sandal feet
kicking through cream
bread and milk
easing mamacita's worries
when the trip is too long
giving up nada

nada
is the contents of the backpack
it's the dark place
            under train wheels
it's eyelashes
            flickering rainbows after tears
            and empty bottle nightmares
            commemorating
            30th street park "take-backs"
it's cash money baseheads
            slangin' promise
            out from floral skirts
            throwing down brown sugar

out the box
it's the stench of dry blood tripas
in store windows
rotting daily
.89 a pound
the slant of vacant lot shadows
abandoned loading docks
turned street cat lean to's
the living circle mass
que quiso tanto
it's red dust
trailing bombas
up graffiti boulevards
and endless laughter
and 32nd street
christ the king crusaders
marching mobs
in the observance
of the wrong ranchero's murder
yields the salt across their backs
but still
ain't about
nada

we best to run home
cuz she's nobody's daughter
so many tattoo tear drops
she looks like a domino
and even when the sun
burns away her heartache
and dime bought afternoon
lies bleeding
in the street
still riding
backward on the east line
sideways from the mainline
running
running
nada into night

it don't mean
niños hide their coins

in converse high tops
just closed eyes
awaiting angels
sleep
  some
    other
      place

THE LOW END

bass was
36 'lo chinos
and a sweatshirt
lamping on an aerosol wall
way passed 2:00 in the morning
you and i
so close to breaking ice
at thirty-three and a third

bass was
bailing after buses
looking like extras from *Juice*
with empty backpacks
tinkling like high hats
screaming
        yo!
           yo!
at the driver not hearing
leaving us just hollering
(cuz something made us want to)
running through cold semesters
with no books
building our knowledge
the way the flows broke down
off album covers
and mario bauzá liner notes
sliding through the meaning
of manteca
taking flicks
        flicks
        flicks
to document us
beaming
young and rugged
up
from the bottom
of forty-fever madness

as we do or die daily
do or die

we were brothers
you
and
i

bass was
"hey chacho
i call you son
because you
shine like one!"
my brother
from another mother
cool
was born
and reborn
nightly

sirens and saxophones
singing
into guarded east side nights
cuz if it wasn't for the music
there would've been no reason
we should have
a place called
home
if it wasn't for the music
we would've never even came with:
"i got love for you,
          i love you man
                    I love you"
or gave up those embraces
we called
"pounds"

if it wasn't for the music
we would've frozen up
in blue funk solitude
passing our last
hieroglyphic breaths
through swisher sweets
it was those beats
it was the music
that made us

do or die daily
do or die
we were brothers
you
and
i

THE URBAN VILLAGE

sky blue
deeper
still water blue
an urban village rising
from the pedestals of pavement
sparking past dark problematic
when mad police cars
swarm past monroe clark
where hamilton has failed

fast turn 42nd at the circus mart
maddox
clocking 1st of the month
check cashing head cracks
knowing you can't buy nothing
without a wic voucher
and a thumb print

                 sign on the x

while pops goes pouring off the top
of similac water dreams
the raids
run toward
the south

our names
ring through
the space of chopper blades
beat senseless
by the tap the cap
beyond
big daddy's broken sky
beat down
by the rustle
of a paper bag
when sidewalks part
red moses
whap the droplets
from wet glass

a monolith in motion
head cocked
eyes locked
deep pockets
sewn

attach the left leg dip sashay
suturing
through asphalt flesh
of body politic
this curbstone walker in the city
with a child at his side
it takes a village
all will say
        a village
        and a father

big daddy slap the back of necks
say who got tommy's boy?
while plates shift
cool tectonics
supersonics
on the jb's tip
his finger whip
sexto sentido
out of 8 tracks

       this is a man's world

introduction
to dominions
that just
take
take
take
and give the rest
a new name
a man
in name only

       boy stop all that mess
       2-pac can't help you now
           you on your own

this proclamation issued
with the crackhead crash
against a mailbox
fighting for the pay phone
wondering
who he s'posed to call
shoulda called somebody
a long time ago
cuz he's tore down
beneath the deafening weight
of countless days assed out
but man enough
to get caught up

> *say what*
> *say what*
> *say what*
> *say what?*

can't hear
the minute
dime drops in it
locked up
tighter than loose change
doled out
by believers

even the stars
come second hand
dropped lovingly
from overhead choppers
blocking out the moon

big daddy
lifts his prayers with them
cuz they say
a child shall lead them

EMERALD HILLS
A PSALM FOR WILLIE JONES

let the news come quiet as it's kept
shabby suede boots fall silently
like breath
but not to carry him away
they wrestle with the caskets
toward organ burials by moonlight
and all that sleep and dream
they cage into a moment
a fingernail space
for just night's peace
they are walking with the caskets
toward becoming
        already becoming

twice this week
the cameras blur
the street color blue

a love supreme

lingering in picket signs
and rolls of yellow tape
masking the mouths
sealing the prayers in protest gospels
dying in tongues
in psalms for willie jones
for mother's sons
and sweaty cop patrol cars
circling the pool

when young men plunged
the stark sunlight wavered
and swung through the neighborhood
from top to bottom
jordan broke
ten thousand miles from itself
and caught their lashes
soaking through the clothes
and darkening the water

like reflections on a porcelain sky

when the first shots came
abdomens whipped inside out
seeping down tearless sidewalks
in a slow parade of bodies
diving into one another
bodies floating through the air
suspended from the sky
resisting
in a
red and black
repose

COLONIA LIBERTAD
GIRL ABOVE THE FLOODPLAIN

indigo
not smiling
ink and tatooed palm
an oracle
a horse and cart
the wind a pendulum
glancing backward
up bareheaded hillsides

indigo
a smoking mirror
winking naked at the sun
a walker's song
below tierra
as the rains begin
a wound remains
untended

indigo
bloodletting
padre kino
lincoln
sanchez taboada
glorietas launch the heroes
from adobe espadaña
campanita clara
a vessel speaking mildly
to warm water rivers
que a veces huelen a cafe

SHELLTOWN
IN WALKED BUD

tonight
the swollen tongue
accepts an easy silence
last breath
spat
recycled from monk requiems
always
already
moving
from melody to skin
from letting out infection
shooting clean night trains
down artery tracks

       on the daily
       in walked bud

       lemme sweep the sidewalk tino
       lemme see the broom

cuz sweeping sidewalks
was like making up his bed
for a five dollar bill
and cold chicken wings
see bud
is what they might call
disillusioned

one foot still in saigon
and the other nailed down
to cold concrete
he mumbles his own mantras
for a pocket full of ones

       i gotta exhale
       cuz we all in hell

reeking degradation and allegory
underneath the liquored breath

and here not for the ages
just the aged
as I offer him some water
bud just breaks it down for me

> *boy, this life is simple*
> *you turn right*
> *and you go straight*

straight?
into grace at attention
tending sidewalks out on tre-deuce
never righting all the candles
drowning in their own faith

so darkness comes down
dark prayers leak
into commercial street masses
for a dollar-fifty boarding pass
to lazily take note
of people
passing
over

a handful of old mourners
gathers at the door
of christ the king

but down the street
around the way
new services take place
on memorial park benches
where bud got blessed
a capful at a time
his name a wave of liquor
pools beneath the tables
like the hustler's easy substitute
for tears
they pass his memory around the cipher
in brown bag communion
alternating sympathy and shame
for the occasional
i told you so

i knew that fool was through
when i seen him the other day
he wasn't about nothing
but messing with that stuff
you can't tell me
you thought bud was gonna make it
and i ain't sorry

a nervous moon
peeps through the trees
lighting the park
that's never quiet after dark
no matter how many cruisers
cruise by in the night

in the dark
the people share
bad meat
and cool company
and listen for the helicopters
lighting up
the alley trap pursuits
as decathletes mob through
on trash dumpster track meets
on a steeplechase
of corrugated mattresses
and glass resin pipes
a moving symphony
sounds like

my life my life
my life my life
in the sunshine
everybody loves the sunshine

he struggles to show heart
on heartless evenings
and the cars move by
not noticing
waiting for that daylight
to clear the dust in circles
over bud
in the empty parking lot

with the cardboard he had found
to collect our trash in
covering his head
over bud
who will not come
to sweep the street
tomorrow

in walked bud
not even his words
will rest easy
on a xico like me
resetting valedictions
and bent
hard out of habit

in walked bud

what monk paints in my headphones
cannot harmonize away
the scene of seeping blood
rooster red
rotting cheeks
supporting idle vessels and beard

as bud releases with the changes
on pulse stops
on pavement blurs
on iron bottle breath
while i recoil
into remote dawns
and listen
for the chest fall
not
repeating

BARRIO LOGAN
UNDER THE BRIDGE

once the day is over
and the booths are cleared away
and sweet asphalt dots its canvas with lunch remains
and warm soda spills from red plastic cups
and children will still play here
on the patch of grass between the traffic lanes
and all will find their ways into the quiet of not being
of owed houses
and $400 rented rooms
and families pushed in
and nothing but the stage remains
amid the echoes of danzantes
and the glint and gleam of chrome wheels
and gone will be the incense pushers
and guatemalan handbags
no tamale stands
no sunglasses
and the street will suck up sticky residues
where hard rocks made their way
between the doñas

once the day is over
and the houses are full
and we are done with ritualistic handshakes
and we remove the smoke and feathers
and only logan can recall who logan is
and recollection seldom comes correct
and looks no longer looks
but just declined invitations to the desperate
and the cops will ponder peace
and billboards will take effect
and the traffic lights will hold true
and the roads will run clear
and the painted princesses will once again be cholas
and the park will not be safe
and the stages will spread out
and barrio will yet
be barrio again

ENCANTO
NEW ALPHA MALES HOUSE PARTY 1992

aloud and sleepless
all but lapsed

though beds be washed away
temptations of deep water
erase all explanations

imminent
dismissal of the body

she released

a daughter
fighting gravelled
saturday night

in self
shunning
brotherhood of she
new alpha she
a fog
a wisp of dickies denim

taken down
a bottle slipped
the black sky
swirling
deep and desperate

forming her reflection
silence
piercing
what is in her color

the stakes get high
more raza talk
familia
still more movement
call concilios

still more movement
still
no
blame

PLAZA BOULEVARD
PALMER WAY SCHOOLYARD HIT-AND-RUN

a mass of dark hair
tangled into ribbons
a wave of eyes
glistening
under butterfly fans
a tide
ebbing
toward saturday
and dulce bulging pockets
stained
from orange
y saladitos

a school hallway
and the wisp of twirling leaves
trapped within a pirouette
where none-too-discrete chambailanes
bow politely
to blame
where cholos in waiting
mouth the lyrics of the matrix
separating seed
from need
hearts beating
in now never time
a waltz of whirling leaves
across gray concrete

a rush
away from recess
and the double dutch gone bad
where noon-time acrobats
turned cartwheels
and called eachother names
like ill sent clouds
descending
on the prayer songs
exiting
their mother's dreams

a rush
down asphalt gangplanks
into silent seas
still pirated away
the weeping waters
young
familiar

racing
in a rush of error and innocence
toward voices
rising to receive them
in the center of a pain sealed place
toward the soft night music
of the womb within
grandmother's memory
toward the vibrant mist
bajando del cielo
in a fog of dusty questions
about future
about failure
about why
and for a moment
all the traffic
starts to stall
between the meeting
of the silence
and the flowers

ESCONDIDO
IRIGOYA'S BENEDICTION

On Wednesday, July 5, 2000 70 year-old Anastasio Irigoya and four other Mexi-can migrant workers came under a vicious attack by 8 or more neo-Nazi skin-heads in San Diego's north county. They were beaten with iron pipes, stabbed with a pitchfork and were repeatedly shot with high power pellet guns. San Diego police later arrested 7 juveniles ages 14–17 in connection with the at-tacks.

evergreen will bring
no precious spirits
to black mountains
or a roadside stand
delivered
like a lost bouquet

no roses from the carmel ranch
or airport outlet flower malls
for diligent consumers

call the name of
irigoya
of la paz y chaparral
so close to earth already

children's children
smack last exits
from his wounds
the heady patriots of backroads
drag his body
into a drainage ditch

and still no news

a scar he wears
still forming

y al fin
ellos llegaron por sus flowers
for the table
pero ya no nos miraron
porque sabían
lo que pasó

IMPERIAL BEACH

I. BOYS GO MISSING

the boys jump fences
fractured
in the gust of wind
more than precisely dead
they leap exactly
dance particularly
skillful

dancing over
(that is: alive)
among those fragments
fallen wood
against which
afternoon rests
a little while

sunday was over
a few shouts drifting
by and by
washing sky
a thinning fading weave
awaiting wings
and boys
hang
like little
moving targets
above the fallen
fence

II. BORDER FIELD STATE PARK

milk the fences dry
in grey crossings
begging
always
if
imagined
this
pastoral

crossing

head high water
ocean front
ripping tide

crossing

into dust clouds
springing
still
not moving
only looming
front to back

go back
across
effete and desolate
america

not threatening
not warning

     que te vayas pues
     pero voy a llegar primero

under shoe and stone
gently
sloping
like long shadows
desecrating

destination
only
too abrupt
on flat plateau
in dark
obstreperous
night

where
there is nothing
but return
and you imagine
not to go
not to search
through useless pockets
to let what is
ungodly
be

EAST VILLAGE WEST
TAQUERO REFLECTIONS UPON LEAVING

i take one last look around
the radio towers
the hills
the brown-eyed girl
set fire
canyons burned
a puff
from baby lungs
gone bad

the unofficial border
at imperial ave.
just brown and black
stood four wide lanes apart
the literal train tracks
crossed us both
no wrong
or right
side

the arteries of our escape
slow transport
from the euclid station
downtown
ghettoscapes

we'd pass the cemetery first
a daily visitation
on to city college come-ups
18 units worth of government loan checks
we called
capital

defaulted early
cuz we liked the taste
of our own shit too much

so money flew into late rent checks
and babylon classes

learning how to write
like meditation in reverse
through lectures
of our discontent
we pushed
toward the water's edge
beneath the star of india's
parade of lights
the tide
drawing ever so near

we made saints
of homeless heroes
found an angel
in the haitian woman
launched herself
off C st. Y
before they'd force her home

we made long days on 16th st.
last through gaslamp underbellies
gilbert blowing faces into stone
in the calm orange glow
the smoke
the unchecked laughter
haciendo gritos
through waging war
with landlords
who'd deny the homes we'd built
under the vaguest of dreams
despite the junkies' ghosts
machine shop workers
lonely spirits
at their windows
into all of this we woke

a ghostly dream
of all downtown proportions
understanding broadway
as our spine

we flipped off front st.
faced our nightmares

at the B st. holding tank
took heart

i know
i'm sayin

it's not me
just the greyhound sign
1st avenue
she's flickering her eyes at me
and luring me
away

THE MISSION
HAND OVER HAND

hands become like 6:00a.m.
where seconds wait
to perforate the day
and we touch morning

our finger-tipped tumbao
above the odd refrain of days
that angle toward the sun
that measure out
her moment of creation

she took licorice roots
and sage leaves
wrapped in purple cord
wove sunrise into cowry shells and feathers
plastered onto yellow walls

she scraped time across a palm leaf
draped its branches
over wooden floors
creaking with absent footsteps
offered water to untold desire
and called it
woman

she built altares
in the hours under eyelashes
and lives rested on cheekbones
brushed her hair away
from afternoon embrace
and carved flint crescents
with her fingers there
at 6:00a.m.
as now
hand over hand
new sign
of peace
and
silence

Mission

THE MOVEMENT
FREESTYLES FOR THE DYING SUN

movement
march
panzón to guitarrón
and liquify p-funk
maintain
norteños mas allá
vicente fernandez
chilling in his b-boy stance
talking trash about
"que de raro tiene"
     no
es mas raro que tenemos
tony lamas
timbos
tripping
ain't no half stepping
in the movement

mariachi muse(sic) riffs
against the twilight
of an olmec head nod
hands fly
flecha fast
to dominate the plate
rotating in the dark
obsidian
outcast on the remix
overrun
by selva sagrada
con su machete
en la mano
mascarada

"nosotros,
hombres y mujeres
íntegros y libres,
estamos conscientes
de que la guerra que declaramos
es una medida última

pero justa"

but don't call it a comeback
we still got mobs of modern macehuales
moving
at the acceleration of gravity
meditating on the microcosm
of the 12-inch
buried mirrors
more than they can stand
who-riding
in a county van

movement
in the middle of caras perdidas
un homenaje
al pasaje
suroeste
where pilot pens
don't take to vinyl
where they need
to draw the line
where the morning left
a midnight of our migration
on a dance floor

damn,
you mean there's four sacred directions
and all that ceremony shit?
yo, i might have to

> *take two and pass*
> *take two and pass*
> *take two and pass*
> *won't get off my ass*

the movement
finds a moment in repose
a mass
unanswered prayer
of signs and sirens
break beats
booming off a red sun

caught
between the upkeep
and the downstroke
movimiento
or moving momentos
on a 45
waxing
oh-no-myth-opaeic
when the needle hits the groove
old heads still
bouncing to the bank
close to the real estate

movement
spins 360
freeze
let the beat drop
into uprock
leaning
toward the center
of ciphers come lately
flair kick
scissor slicing
hooded heads
with ash
and empty bottles
running
off the r.p.m.

movement
measured in the line length
of a freestyle
for the dying sun
a rough face
leapt into the lyric
ticking
tongue glyphs
up the temple steps
rhyme
from reed songs
rolling
>   *to the east*
>   *my brother*

to the east

where the whole house
bounce to rooftops
and the sky
begins
brand new

so you can
throw your hands to the sky
and wave em
from side to side
but if you came here
to spark up the movement, y'all
you better get here
fo' the whole thing dies

MISSION REDUX

mission manifesto
made redux
reprise
re-use
mash on
an under-echelon
of epitaphs
made murals

tore down
our niche beneath potrero
on a smokestack colored morning
and the children
off to school
there was a bell
teacher remembers
antiseptic anthems
over antithetic rubrics
and better still
the children come
on foot
with infantile arrogance
they come
with tablets and with pencils
empty baskets
built for hesitation
built for limbs etched out
in light and concrete
wounds
replace the wombs
of mother's lungs
exquisite time
on tongues
cut taken
this ephemera
that shimmers
on the glassy eyes of children
running
raging
into no one's dying light

beyond the clasping of their lashes
shutting out
the flowing visions
of shared bedrooms
and a dusty kitchen table

these
they will not sacrifice
as lids grip tighter
over memory and place
displaced
the new beginnings
of old endings
where the stop and go days
last longer
than the curse of shattered mirrors

dreams
reflected of themselves
retreating
into multiplicity
made history
of hunger
and invisible arms
locked into barely felt embrace
a face
that time will never know
seeking
over ever-present mounds
from last night's eviction
cast off
by many mourners
holding hands
maintaining ranks
solidified
by
silence

somedays
the children
reach out
on paper white shirtsleeves
trailing blue bandera uniforms

through cancer causing breeze
so many
kites without tails
sin ganas de volar
emerging wings
already clipped
become the fall
of western wal mart
ridden
by the complex schemes
of 99¢ shopping
on the lowlands
of a highbrow culture

> *mission manifesto*
> *made redux*
> *reprise*
> *re-use*
> *mash on*
> *the under-echelon*
> *of epitaphs*
> *made murals*

on mission street
at noon
between the traffic cones
and overdue construction
beyond the solace of a bus bench
girl goes pushing
pushing into sweaty days
jalando
tres generaciones
wearing faded chivas jersey

the markers
more the milestones
have moved so far
from making sense
because she
cannot speak the language
she just
looks with rage
imbedded within

the inability to look
to sing
the song and psalms of looking
at ourselves
in equal measure
we see buddha
and ritchie valens

call them scars
as we been tongue lashed
through the ages
the first word
become an epilogue
forbidden
from the dialogue
we marinate
on tax breaks
watching weary arms
tow children
toward september
when school begins
and language
becomes pretense
disaggregate delusion
a satchel we keep tugging
through television windows
like linguistic thieves at night
ready to pocket the silver
and render
english
unto caesar

born
with the sun
in our mouths
become a hummingbird swarm
pinned
to the collar of an unwashed shirt
like a note
sent home from teacher
bearing
the standards
like illuminated manuscripts

kids read
only
the pictures
wringing palabras from
soaking garments
straight white-washed
in the translation
but hanging on the line
we fail
only
the children

isn't it all
just so
familiar?
            how even
            their silence
            has a vibration

            how rhetoric
            subsides

            how in the interim
            we pause
            and hold our breath
            over millennia

            one thousand one
            one thousand two
            one thousand three

CUANDO GANAMOS

shadows of the new forreal
fall sixty stories
over antique row apartments
where victoria runs crooked
under late victorians

dipping from the sloping sun
making room
for undone renovations
and the sprawl
of this new street
maintaining
life
above its own

your town
my town
anytown usa

there's no
new
here
no
viable
no
cradle of the crescent
only
after-school unrest
a rumored peace
without
the decency
of truthtelling

we
armed only
with obsessions for silence
and for waving hands
say
get your hands up
get your hands in the air

but can't stop
the double-dip parlays
at the corner stores
where the homies chill
in lawn chairs
the unknown warriors
that lean
un
steadily
against a mural
of their own fifth sun

as if we'd need a reason
to subdue the urges
of our exodus
the exegesis
spilling
onto sidewalks
where the old gods
are remembered
and you just
can't step there blood

this said
through telepathic logic
and the passing of a paper bag
where we spit
40-ounce foam,
and roll up
on the unsuspecting destiny
of power lines
and patrol cars
ever clocking
as the world
has shrunk to
this

from the moment we left dreaming
left with
leering sadness
sleeping
on street corners
stoops

have stooped too low
enduring the weight
of everyday absolution

in the poem
we must name
the hottest corners
that we've been through
this
the willing traces
of our pens
across the pavement
corners
leaning
against lampposts
where the malos
carry on with markers
at artilleries
of old strategic planning
and the myths
that are good citizens
have taken their good will
toward our center
we see
socrates
holding a vial
at 24th
and mission

where the mangoes
drip from traffic lights
grown weary
in the haze of grey saturdays
and pulsing cars
line up
to start the plucking
at the intersection

those on foot survey
so many rows of luggage racks
lining sidewalks
for a population bent
on traveling home

always departing
as they arrive
in ten dollar duffel bags
with pockets lined
with telegiros
and lotto tickets
scratching
at the chances
for return

>*a una isla encantada*
>*a una montaña en centroamerica*
>*a un rancho lindo y lejos*
>*de este pueblo congelado*

unreachable
those mangoes
should the traffic lights
through civic sympathy or shame
allow their frozen fruit
to fall at 24th street
we would dive
within the skin and pulp
before they even
hit the pavement
beyond the fleshy fiber strands
the meat
beyond original confusion
we would fight
to find the pit of fruitless searches
for beginnings
but fruit's not gonna fall
and sympathetic poets
don't fertilize fool
and you ain't growin no trees

>*bueno 'mano*
>*si quieres mangos*
>*vamos al chinito güey*

so we hit the spot
pop the top
on nectars come in cans

like the essence
that is us-sense
chillin in the coolers
of chinito's corner store
where old drunks
slanted sideways
on a $50 million jackpot dream
play lotto
and complain about
la renta

they'll take their crumpled tickets home tonight
the numbers plucked
from memories and shame
tonight
someone behind a tv tray
within a damp apartment
will tune in to anticipate
the call of
birthdates
children's ages
days since their arrival
street addresses
fake social security numbers
saints days
bible passages
years when they were happy
and even those will not appear
will not deliver
out their random race through time
toward the going back
to leave them
quietly needing
in the dark

> *bueno 'mano*
> *cuando ganamos*
> *te compro mangos*

fuck that bro
if we win
i'm buyin you
some mangoes

ORIGINAL
TO BE GIVEN TO
THE PERSON NATURALIZED

CERTIFICATE OF

Petition No. 73271

Personal description of holder as of date of naturalization
complexion Dark color of eyes Brown
weight 147 pounds; visible distinctive marks Non
Marital status Single
I certify that the description above given is tru

sign here

(SECURELY AND PERMANENTLY
AF

(TH
SO

EDGE OF THE PHOTOGRAPH)

Aniceto Medina

Seal

UNITED STAT
SOUTHERN DIST

Be it kno
then residing
having petition
a term of the--

the court havin
United States, he
States in such c
ordered that the

In testim
day of A
f
and s

No. 4998152

NATURALIZATION

41 _years. sex_ Male _color_ Brown

hair Black _height_ 5 _feet_ 3½ _inches._

former nationality Filipino

that the photograph affixed hereto is a likeness of me.

PART 4
MAHCIC

i ceto Medina

complete and true signature of holder

MERICA ⎫
IFORNIA ⎬ _s.s:_

** ANICETO MEDINA **

S."SARATOGA", San Pedro, California

admitted a citizen of the United States of America, and at

District _____ _Court of_ ____ The United States ____

_____ _held pursuant to law at_

geles _____ _on_ AUG 9 1940 _19_

that the petitioner intends to reside permanently in the

respects complied with the Naturalization Laws of the United

able and was entitled to be so admitted, the court thereupon

to be admitted as a citizen of the United States of America.

of the seal of the court is hereunto affixed this 9th

in the year of our Lord nineteen hundred and

and of our Independence the one hundred

ifth.

R. S. Zimmerman

Clerk of the ____ U. S. District ____ _Court._

_By_ Murray E. Fire _Deputy Clerk._

MAHCIC:
A MEXIPINO GENEALOGY

I.   GRANDMA PEARL'S HUMMING SONG

harmonizing daily over
church songs
some begotten
some forgotten
some frustrated hymns
all echoing
cuts east
at 33rd just near imperial
the church
the trolley station
channels for the freeway run-off
and a freedom school mural

all of this
and grandma hums
never moving her lips

> *i may not know the words*
> *but i can damn sure sing the song*

grandma say
our will above all others'
say it late in life
the growth upon her chest
what she say
remembrance even
spirit sagging
dangerously right
undone
our will
raised
just to endure

born into precarious
indignation
into unexpected urgency
a rush through explanations

through miscegenation riot
left the fighting and the bluegrass hills
behind her

carved a color unto herself
the yellowbrown girl
wash insoluble
wrought family's desecrated rightness
cut off at the knees

her tongue
serrated
like a walking tide
washes away its burden
a spirit moved
a voice of moments
missed

       next time
she hums
       next time
       next time
       next time

II.   GRANDPA FLOATING HALFWAY HOME

grandpa aniceto
born to die at sea
to tear up at the sky
to rush the wind

a battleship and promises
mark his citizenship address
he dons formal attire for the photo
trembling slightly
where the camera
cannot see

now floating home
bereft
on luscious wave caps
rocking body
softly
toward the surface

      finally
      his elevation

rising over sunken ship
his stateside children
staring fatherless moments in the face
and floating
like the ice-cubes in the glass
at the one bar in town
that served him
where he learned to love
his other

III.   AFTER TELEGRAM DAY

her coffee cup
hangs idly
next to his
from a hook
beneath the cupboard

long time
summer afternoons
leave avocado picking
empty chicken coops
and bourbon
leave her house alone
his car still in the driveway

IV.   SHE HAD TO

she had to come
through whisky breath
and slim silhouetted after-hours
the way she came to know
the last call
serving
she came home to do
she served him

she had to

might just call herself
alone
buoyed and laughing
caught up
in the current of all currents

she had to come
through accidents
defiance
and the widow
sobbing softly

she had to fight step-father
through the doorway
chucking her chuck taylor's
and the deal to live at home
her backbone fixed to run away

she had to find herself
to lose herself
balboa park
the museum chimes and fountain
vague and so of man
that man alive with her at hand
accrued a lifetime of memories
one afternoon
found flaking eucalyptus groves
a windsong
carrying fruit wine away

an ordered pair apparent
err a parent
ordering perpetual withdrawal
no son would have her
she would have son
in air
his sign
her earth
a paradox
calmly beneath it all
the son and heir

she had to call out in her sleep
into the brilliant ocean of light
marking this birth
making the day
order his name
to separate his limbs from hers
pour water on the tendons
bind the myth back to her bones
take shape again

she had to

V.   GOOD NEIGHBORS

she drinks now
more than she did before
writes me letters
all in lower case

i call them letters
as i recall her parker
and the steno pad
i wasn't allowed to write in

     to be 5

late night
when her man climbs
through a window
with his brother

     if anything happens
     go get your auntie
     otherwise get up and go to school
     like i was here

she's older now
hair no longer than her shoulders
wishing for her back
longing to brush her waist again

she lights her menthol gpc
on my back porch and coughs
a shudder running through her
coughs again

i move to close the door
she says
     baby
     you won't do this around him?
nods because i've quit
she coughs again
exhaling smoke
seraphic

he held her down
and pinned her arms back
with his knees
as he reached down between them
for her throat

his brother laughed
he watched him choke her

the bed we shared alive
the coughing and the screaming
boring into us

i don't know who called you
i said we were just playing

on my back porch
she's only thinking
of the baby
not the time
the neighbors
saved her life

VI.   MY BROTHER'S NAME

he knew only
he was second born
and so i answered
older brother cool
cut patronym
sí «sans» patrón

your name
and mine
we called him (father)
yet will not be called

be patronized
placated
once and always
it's just
syllables

his syllables
won't name you

VII.   THEY TOLD US WE NEEDED JESUS

the sisters prayed
with scented angels
chorus of our curls
behind them

they bore no scripture
wrought no new beginning
brought no clemency
or pious moments

left us arms out on a concrete sea
in a cinder block
box canyon
anxious
nameless
stuck in the belligerence
of birthrights
with just his blood
his needing nothing
primacy
point taken

pretty faces
all upturned
sentient
deserving
standing on a land mine
in the moment
in this moment
in the thousand drunken hours
looking upward to denial
to deny him
to defy soliloquies and silhouettes
called family

deny him
as the prophets and the scholars
turn the page
and we

stay still
we
family

we aching fragments
searching for a face

VIII.   REMOVING HIS BODY

men voice to voice
bent low-speaking
him now surely locked
right in the middle of fire and all
slow circling in the hallway
saw no spirit
slip away

and we watched him
swaddled in chemist wraps
two hands at each end
carried him out
by his dull joints
through wordless non-exchanges
over whisper and memory
and nicotine trauma
and lips not uttering
and passing unremembered
and the unprodigious swell
of all unkempt houses
stuck
pretending
to be born

IX.　　REMEMBERING THE FAMILY PORTRAIT

just to awaken
our uncertain faces
with the chill
that says
we lived
and were

small and tumultuous
tired
unassuming
fashioned
in absentia

>   he almost crashed the car
>   on our way to olan mills
>   to take the family portrait
>
>   gran torino
>   skirting off the road
>   skidding through the ivy
>   just missing the guardrail
>
>   spinning
>   family
>   screaming

our faces
would always look that way
like they did
in the picture
we took that day

we placed it
on the mantle
in the house
he kept us in

X.   YOU DIDN'T COME GENTLY

Do not go gently into that good night.
Rage, rage against the dying of the light.
-Dylan Thomas

a ritual of long nights
stretched through darkness
raging only from this
fatherly advice

as i say
           breathe
willing your body
see me
pushing down the trail
between
rebellion and denial
dry as all out want
for both the blessing and the lost cause
for empirical relief
from legs that just won't genuflect
from sunrise
dragging on toward your arrival

           do not go gently

           as if we got a choice
           we fighting just because
           one death, one thousand deaths
           we come back
           despite death
           no light
           no warnings
           rising
           unafraid

western deities
and pragmatists love fear
but new sons
they love fathers
love the tough love from the nose

down to the chin
and feel no end there
call it faith
a lifetime exorcising father
lost in this since i was eight
with tender fists
and wont to find my mother
nodding
always
nodding
no need for explanation
or for language
and nobody sang up through
the valley of the sparrow

    you will die
    and you don't want to die

    some prophecies ring true
    or through you
    tell a child this
    in this elevated language
    damn the poets

it was not enough now
not enough warm
not enough beginning
not to be checking at my back
for brawny paper towel chested america

my son was coming up
my arms had become bristles
through my coat
there wasn't no we yet nowhere
meaning me and him
and dylan thomas looked as crooked
as the shrinking woman shuffle
for a quarter on 22nd saturday night

call him crooked as he oughta be
    sometimes
    ought not to be
    no poets

XI.   THIS IS WHAT IT BE LIKE

your drunk uncle will call
and be surprised to know your name again
your grandmother will call
after your birthday
nobody at the doorway with a
no solicitors mat
that's just family

it's the loud talk
your mama's ailing hands
and more loud talk

but nobody's gonna call the law
to get no poets out the discourse
ain't nobody bout to bring back
grandpa monroe
or shine the light two generations back
for aniceto
see the call
become non-sequitor
the call be oxymoron

       family history

a confession for too small communities
yes we're troubled too
a demographic affirmation
adding zeroes to the decimal
       the decimate
       disseminate
       dissension in the ranks
       cuz nothing's easy
       nothing's safe
       nothing's free
lesson:
one night
they mugged a woman on our block
they dragged her by the purse strings to the street
i ran down to help her
despite knowing if i was her

fur collar no
gucci purse no
cole heels no
i wouldn't have been me there
here

i ran down the stairs to help her
caught burnt tires
but no thieves
she was alright
scared
but surprisingly
unappreciative

cops ask can you describe them?
i have to say

> *"white car ford, crown victoria*
> *four black no, african american males*
> *no license plate they were gone before i could get it*
> *yo, but that don't mean i want you to go bust*
> *every black dude with a white car in the mission"*

she assured me that they wouldn't
though nothing any cop has ever said to me
has set my mind at ease
no sense explaining

cuz they hardly know me
but they already know you
they already have a spotlight
created in your image

a silhouette hands up
or on its knees
fingers clasped tightly
like to hold it down or
like to hold your head together
in the one place
you'll be guaranteed a stage

you will be
composing half-bilingual rhymes

on juri commons swing sets
when that light will shine
or
crawling through the sand
at baker beach
when lights will shine
in opposite degrees
a shade beneath you
dimming your skin tone
again

so shine within

your skin be
just this color
would it also
be so thick
the day
you shift your tongue
to ask me

is it true?

XII. AN ANSWER

there are no answers
to not being
just a scream that never stops
and i will tell you
scream m'ijito scream
            grandma pearl blues
            and salsa spirituals
scream the lure of water
the power of moonlight
the secret sense of dippity doo and blood

scream against arched eyebrows
and your marked canela skin

twist your artful body's masterpiece
to scream above the burning
scream til you can't take it
then you take it to the head

you take it
use it
live
fight
pray

as you make sacred
our transition from the wrecked world
to the next world
cuz now i get it m'ijo
i've done all of this
for you

About the Author

Tomás Riley is a poet, writer, educator and a veteran of the seminal Chicano spoken-word collective The Taco Shop Poets. A finalist for the 2004 California Voices Award from *Poets & Writers Magazine*, his written work has been featured in *Bum Rush the Page: A Def Poetry Jam, Chorizo Tonguefire: The Taco Shop Poets Anthology, Pacific Review* and various journals and literary publications. His extensive performance history has brought him into venues nationwide in a continuing proactive effort to bring Chicano spoken word to relevant spaces. Currently he mentors teen writers as the Youth Development Program Director at Youth Speaks, a non-profit literary arts organization for young people in San Francisco.

Author's Note/Acknowledgements

This book, which began as a simple punctuating statement for my tenure with The Taco Shop Poets, has taken on new meaning since the arrival of our son Mahcic in November 2004. He shares his name with the title and vice versa, but the truth be known, the title came first. How apropo, two poets name their son after a book and his arrival becomes metaphor: completion. That said, the tie between the two of them demanded more direct correlation, after all, the book now bears the child's name. Somehow the book should earn that right, and the final piece in this collection is an attempt at just that–an extended "family history" documenting his ancestors through his poet-father's imperfect memory written with the explicit wish to guide him forward with an understanding of his past. This is more than a dedication.

Deepest appreciation goes out to all of you who have supported me in this work: Leticia Hernández, Anthony, Matthew, Denise, Mom–we're all survivors, Adrian Arancibia, Miguel-Angel Soria, Adolfo Guzman Lopez, ThaiMex, Cameron Jasper, Nick Carvajal, Andy Burton, Angel Nevarez, Michael Figgins, Kevin Green, Zopilote, The 740 Collective, El Campo Ruse, The Voz Alta Project, Gary Ghirardi, Stephanie de la Torre, Pat Payne, Willie Perdomo, Marisela Norte, raúlrsalinas, Genny Lim, Bennie Herron, Jahsun Edmonds, Brent Beltrán, Consuelo Manríquez, Bill Nericcio, Sulaiman, Diego Davalos, Izcalli y el Circulo de Hombres, Ariel Robello, Lizz Huerta, Gilbert Castellanos, Mike Kamoo, Paul Espinosa, Ricardo Griswold del Castillo, Emily Hicks, Marilyn Chin, Adelaida del Castillo, Poetry Television, Tropico de Nopal, Galería de la Raza, Jimi Salcedo Malo, Marc Pinate, Paul Flores, Jason Mateo, James Kass, Joan Osato, Kahlil Peebles, Marc Bamuthi Joseph, Aimee Suzara, Mush Lee, Ise Lyfe, Lauren Wingate and the entire Youth Speaks Family, and all my relations past and present–¡Mil Gracias!